D1243236

# ECOSYSTEMS

## Life in a
# Pond

### Stuart A. Kallen

**KIDHAVEN
PRESS™**

**THOMSON**

**GALE**

San Diego • Detroit • New York • San Francisco • Cleveland
New Haven, Conn. • Waterville, Maine • London • Munich

**LIBRARY OF CONGRESS CATALOGING-IN-PUBLICATION DATA**

Kallen, Stuart A., 1955-
 Life in a pond / by Stuart A. Kallen.
  p. cm. — (Ecosystems)
Summary: Explores the pond ecosystem, discussing where ponds are found, how a pond develops, and the interdependence of the plants and animals that live in and around it.
Includes bibliographical references and index.
 ISBN 0-7377-1532-4 (alk. paper)
 1. Pond ecology—Juvenile literature. 2. Ponds—Juvenile literature. [1. Pond ecology. 2. Ponds. 3. Ecology.] I. Title. II. Series.
 QH541.5.P63K34 2004
 577.63'6—dc21
                                                                          2003009408

Printed in China

# Contents

# Chapter 1

# What Is a Pond?

**P**onds are fascinating freshwater communities that teem with wildlife. They play an important role in nature by providing **habitat**—that is, a place to live—for beautiful birds; blood-sucking mosquitoes; fat, croaking frogs; and many other living things. There are millions of ponds in the world and they may be found in many different natural **environments**. Meadows, mountainsides, and even deserts may all be the home to ponds and pond life.

A pond may be thought of as a bog, a swamp, a little lake, or even a giant mud puddle. Some ponds are as big as a city block, while others are as small as the average backyard. There is no scientific definition for these bodies of water, but all ponds have several features in common. Ponds are small and less then ten acres in size—about the same area as ten football fields. Ponds contain **fresh water**, unlike the salt water found in the ocean. With a depth of about four to fifteen feet, ponds are shallow, and the water does not usually make waves. Since sunlight can usually reach the bottom, pond water maintains a uniform temperature throughout. For example, if the water is sixty-five degrees at the surface, it is also sixty-five degrees at the bottom. The temperature of this shallow water changes rapidly with the outside temperature, however, and a pond

*A still pond reflects the mountains that surround it. Ponds appear in many different natural environments, including mountains, forests, and meadows.*

that is sixty-five degrees on a sunny day may cool as much as twenty degrees at night.

Though they are small, ponds are known for their rich variety of plant and animal life. They often contain more **species** than any other watery environment. Unlike lakes and rivers, however, most ponds do not have names.

## Glaciers and Rivers

Although all ponds share similar qualities, they are formed in many different ways. Some of the oldest ponds in the world were made during the last ice age more than ten thousand years ago. At that time mam-

*Forest ponds are often formed by flooding rainwater or melting snow.*

moth blocks of ice called **glaciers** inched across the landscape, scraping holes into the earth. When the glaciers eventually melted away, their icy waters filled the holes and ponds were formed.

Other types of ponds have been created in more recent times. For example, a large river can give birth to a pond in several days when water flowing through a sharp U-shaped bend suddenly changes course and begins to flow in a straight line. This cuts off the loop and leaves an isolated U-shaped basin called an oxbow pond.

A river can also create a pond when rain or melting snow causes the water to overflow its banks during a flood. This floodwater can pool into a series of swampy

ponds in low-lying areas of woods and meadows near the riverbanks. Such ponds can be temporary and disappear within a matter of weeks or months.

## A Variety of Dams

Some ponds are formed overnight when a rockslide, mudslide, or earthquake dumps debris into a small stream and creates a natural **dam**. The flowing river backs up behind this dam and floods the surrounding land, thereby creating a pond.

Not all dams are caused by falling debris, however. In woodland areas in parts of North America, Europe, and Asia, dams are often created by beavers from shrubs and small trees the animals cut down with their sharp teeth. Beavers live within their dams, which have several dry rooms connected by long tunnels. The ponds that back up behind the beaver dams provide habitat for thousands of creatures.

Humans are perhaps the only creatures that can create ponds faster than the busy beaver. Farmers build artificial ponds to provide places for their families to fish and boat and for their livestock to drink and bathe. Cities create ponds in parks so visitors can ride paddleboats in the summer and ice skate in the winter. And large businesses often build ponds on their grounds so workers will have scenic places to relax.

## Ponds Throughout the World

Natural ponds are located nearly everywhere in the world except at the North and South Poles. Rocky

*A beaver dam is visible in this shallow pond. Beavers are just one of the animals that make their homes in ponds.*

ponds created by glaciers are found in the tundra of northern Canada, northern American states such as Minnesota and Wisconsin, and in northern Russia.

Mountainous regions from western Canada to the Himalayas in Tibet are pocked with small alpine ponds nestled in shallow valleys between hillsides. Temporary ponds form during rainstorms in the hot, arid regions of Utah, Nevada, and eastern California in the United States.

In tropical countries such as Thailand and Vietnam, abundant rainfall and hot sun create ponds that are as warm as bath water. These soupy basins provide habitat to an amazing concentration of creatures, from single-celled plants to turtles that weigh up to two hundred pounds.

Ponds are even found in the barren reaches of the Sahara Desert in Africa and the Gobi Desert in central Asia, where temperatures can reach 120 degrees. These water holes, ringed with palm trees, are known as oases (the plural of oasis). They provide water for thirsty people and animals and habitat for insects, frogs, birds, and other wildlife.

## Ponds to Marshes to Bogs

Although a pond often seems like a permanent part of the landscape, it has a life cycle like a plant or animal. Like living **organisms** most ponds are born, live for a time, grow old, and die. This can be seen in the shallow ponds behind beaver dams. These ponds fill in slowly with decaying plants and dirt, called silt, that is carried into the pool by the stream. Within a period of fifty to one hundred years, the pond becomes choked with long cattails, bushes, and shrubs that grow from the shore toward the open water at the center of the pond. As this happens decaying stems, plants, leaves, and branches turn the clear waters thick and brown. Soon trees begin to grow and the dying pond becomes so full of mud and vegetation that

*Ponds provide the habitat for beavers and many other plants and creatures.*

fewer and fewer water-loving plants and animals can survive there. Eventually the former pond becomes just another place in the forest, home to creatures who thrive on dry land.

Although they are often small, shallow, and temporary, ponds play an extremely important role in the natural world. They provide habitat for a complex web of life that includes fish, frogs, trees, lily pads, birds, bugs, and beavers. Their natural beauty has inspired poets and painters while their cool waters attract swimmers on a hot summer's day.

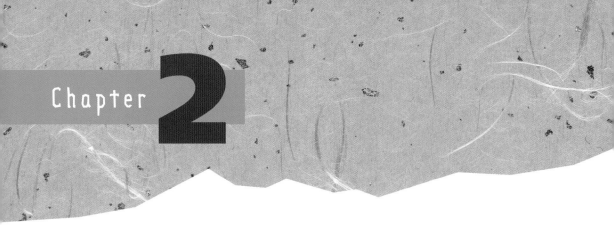

# Chapter 2

# Pond Plantlife

**T**hroughout the world ponds provide a rich habitat in which thousands of plant species float, flower, and reproduce. The seeds, stems, leaves, and roots of these plants supply food for many animals, including fish, frogs, snakes, bugs, birds, squirrels, deer, and even people. In this way every pond is like a lush garden that provides a nearly constant store of food to countless creatures.

Algae are perhaps the most important plants in a pond. They are also the smallest and most numerous. Some species of algae are so tiny that a thousand can fit on the head of a pin and 10 million may be found in only a quart of pond water. These microscopic plants, however, provide many benefits to the pond environment.

Like all plants algae soak up the energy provided by the sun. In a process called **photosynthesis**, algae convert this energy into food and oxygen. All creatures need oxygen to breathe, even if they live in water, and this vital gas is used by plants, fish, and other **aquatic** organisms. Without the oxygen provided by algae, ponds would be barren and lifeless.

Algae can multiply rapidly in waters warmed by the summer sun. When this happens these microscopic plants can fill ponds with large floating masses

*Microscopic algae (inset) convert the sun's energy into food. When algae multiply, they give ponds a dark greenish color (main photo).*

called "blooms." These slimy clumps of algae sometimes emit foul-smelling gases that reek like rotten eggs. They also produce poisons that may be harmful to small animals within the pond.

Algae may be found anywhere in a pond. Larger plants, however, only thrive in certain areas, or zones, within a pond. Scientists have divided ponds into four zones where water depth, temperature, and other factors attract certain types of plants. Whether the pond is in a tropical area or in a cold climate, many of these plant species are common to ponds all over the world.

## The Swamp Zone

Ponds tend to be deepest in the center and slope uphill toward the edges. The swamp plant zone is the area nearest to the shore where the water is shallowest.

The swamp plant zone is covered with water in all but the driest periods of the year. It provides the ideal habitat for tall, upright plants like reeds, grasses, and rushes. These plants, such as reed sweet grass and bulrush, have long, narrow leaves that allow them to remain in sunlight even during times of flooding. Their hollow stems are thick and tough so that they can withstand high winds. These plants reproduce rapidly and create thick beds of vegetation that may extend over large areas of the pond.

Cattails, which can grow up to twelve feet high, are probably the most familiar of all pond plants in this zone. Their swaying, brown, cigar-shaped heads are made up of thousands of tiny flowers tightly packed

# Zones of a Mountain Pond

**① Swamp Zone**
This is the shallowest area of the pond.
Tall upright plants like reeds
and cattails live here.

**④ Free Floating
Plant Zone**
This is the deepest
area of the pond.
Plants such as
the frogbit and the
carnivorous
bladderwort
live here.

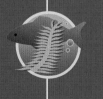

**② Floating Leaf Zone**
The water in this area is
less than five feet deep.
Plants in this zone have
leaves and flowers that
float on the surface
of the water.

**③ Submerged
Plant Zone**
This area's deep
water is home to
plants that live
completely
underwater.

together on top of their stems. During late summer and early fall, these flowers will fall apart and release millions of wispy, cottonlike seeds into the wind.

Over the centuries cattails have been used as food, medicine, and construction material. They are some-times called the "supermarket of the swamp" because in the spring their roots and shoots can be used in sal-ads and stews. In the summer the pollen stalks at the center of the flower heads can be eaten like corn on the cob. And in autumn cattail pollen can be used like flour to cook pancakes and cattail cornbread.

In past centuries Native Americans used cattails for many other purposes. The fluffy seeds were used to stuff pillows and bedding. The dried stalks were made into arrow shafts. The dried stems could be made into baskets, ropes, chairs, hats, and mats. They were even used to weave dome-shaped houses called wigwams.

## The Floating Leaf Zone

Beyond the cattails in the swamp zone, the area with waters three to five feet deep is known as the floating leaf zone. Most of the plants that grow in this zone, such as the water plantain and broad-leaved pondweed, sprout leaves and flowers that float on the water. The roots of these plants grow into the mud at the bottom of the pond.

Beautiful white water lilies are the most common plants found in the floating leaf zone throughout north-ern Europe and North America. These plants have large, greenish-purple leaves with V-shaped notches and large white fragrant flowers throughout the summer.

White water lilies can cover large areas of the pond's surface and are extremely useful to many creatures. Their large leaves provide shade and covering for insects and fish to hide from **predators** such as birds. They also act as landing pads where frogs can bask in the sun.

*Water lilies are a common pond plant. Their broad green leaves provide shade and hiding places for many insects and fish.*

# The Submerged Plant Zone

Near the center of a pond where the water is deeper, plants cannot grow tall enough to spread their leaves over the surface. Although they are rooted in the mud of the pond floor, these plants are **submerged**, that is, they remain underwater at all times. Therefore, this area is called the submerged plant zone.

Plants in this zone, such as the stonewort, water milfoils, and water violet, have a large number of very small leaves that are feathery and thin. Some of these plants are very slimy because they are coated with a mucuslike substance that prevents them from becoming waterlogged.

Plants like the Canadian waterweed add oxygen to the water. On sunny days this plant, the leaves of which float near the surface, converts sunlight into oxygen. This gas, which is necessary to keep aquatic creatures alive, can be seen bubbling to the surface like the fizz in a glass of soda.

# The Free-Floating Plant Zone

While many plants are firmly rooted in the mud of the pond floor, some float freely on top of the water or just below the surface. They often exist in the deepest waters of the pond, an area known as the free-floating plant zone.

Free-floating plants, such as the water hyacinth, frogbit, and water fern, are not rooted in the soil.

*Bladderworts (detail, inset) surround a cypress tree. The bladderwort is a carnivorous free-floating plant that eats small insects.*

Many, however, have hairlike roots that hang down into the water where they are able to absorb minerals and oxygen.

## Bug-Eating Bladderwort

Perhaps the most interesting of the free-floating plants is the bladderwort, with over two hundred species found in Europe, North America, Asia, and northern Africa. Since this plant is found in ponds where there are few **nutrients**, it eats small insects for nourishment. To do this the plant uses small air pockets, called bladders, that are found between the narrow branches of the plant. Each bladder has a small trapdoor in the shape of a funnel with tiny hairs projecting from it. The bladder excretes a foodlike substance to attract insects and other creatures. When they touch the sensitive hairs, the trapdoor snaps shut, snaring the victim within the bladder. The creature dies as the bladder secretes a digestive juice to dissolve it. The plant then absorbs the nutrients.

While the bladderwort is one of the only meat-eating plants in a pond, all plants have developed their own unique methods of survival. Whether firmly rooted near the shore or lazily floating in the center, pond plants are joined into an important web of life. Within this connected environment, thousands of organisms can eat, breed, and thrive.

# Chapter 3

# Creatures of the Pond

On a sunny summer day, a pond looks like a peaceful place. Brightly colored dragonflies dart above the calm waters, birds sing in the bushes, and turtles sun themselves on logs. Looks are deceiving, however, and ponds are anything but peaceful. In fact, ponds are some of the most extreme environments on Earth, a place where hundreds of hungry creatures are always on the hunt. In this "eat or be eaten" world, fish gobble down insects, birds swoop down and grab the fish, and turtles chomp down on frogs that are too slow to escape.

In this web of life and death, all creatures are connected by what is called the food chain. That is, the smallest organisms are eaten by larger ones, and those

21

are consumed by even bigger creatures. For example, tiny shrimp are eaten by small sunfish. The sunfish are swallowed by frogs, small birds, and larger fish such as bass. These animals, in turn, fall prey to the largest meat eaters in or around the pond, such as snapping turtles, hawks, raccoons, and otters.

## Skaters and Divers

Ponds are home to hundreds of species of slithering, swimming, and flying insects. Some live in or on the

*Ponds are home to many kinds of insects, including this backswimmer bug.*

water, others fly above it. Water striders, or pond skaters, are insects that glide on top of the water. Unlike most insects that have claws, pond skaters have tiny tufts of hair on the ends of their legs that allow them to walk on water. These bugs can often be seen devouring dragonflies and other insects that have accidentally fallen into the pond.

While pond skaters float like pontoon boats, whirligig beetles swim crazily around in circles like spinning tops. This playful behavior, however, ends when the whirligig begins its search for food.

There are over eleven hundred species of whirligig beetles, and they are found in countries throughout the world including Australia, Great Britain, Canada, and the United States. Whirligigs can hunt both on the surface of the water and underneath it.

With eyes that are divided into two halves, the beetle can peer into the air and into the water at the same time. When small insects fall into the water, the whirligig uses its wide legs to "row" over to eat it. When it wants to hunt below the surface, like a submarine, the insect can grab a bubble of air between its back wings and use it to breathe while underwater. When the beetle finds a tadpole or small fish, it injects a poison into it that turns the victim's inner organs into liquid. The whirligig then sucks the juice out of its prey.

# Blood Drinkers

While the whirligig kills its victims, mosquitoes drink the blood of living creatures. There are over

*Thousands of insects, such as this water bug, make their home on the surface of ponds.*

twenty-seven hundred species of mosquitoes, and they can be found buzzing around ponds from the tropical rain forests of South America to the glacial ponds in the far northern regions of Russia. While the male eats all sorts of things, from flower nectar to decaying plants, female mosquitoes need blood from living creatures to develop eggs. After delivering bites and storing the blood, a female mosquito may lay up to three thousand eggs in her one-hundred-day lifetime. The insect needs standing water to lay her eggs, and the edges of ponds provide a perfect habitat for these vampires to reproduce. Unfortunately, when mosquitoes bite they inject a venom into the victim. This causes the bite to itch. It also can spread deadly diseases such as malaria.

# Underwater Hunters

Some of the only creatures safe from mosquito bites are fish. These underwater swimmers, however, are constantly preying on one another.

Most visitors to ponds can see schools of tiny minnows darting through the waters. While many

*A fishing spider makes a meal of a reed frog. Frogs and spiders are natural enemies, each preying on the other.*

minnow species are only about one inch long, some, such as squawfish and carp, can grow up to four feet long and weigh up to fifty pounds. Although these large fish are of the same family as the small minnows, the big fish eat the little ones in large numbers.

Even fat carp have to beware of members of the pike family, considered the most ferocious fish in a pond. From the foot-long pickerel to the large northern pike, these fish are the sharks of the pond. Long and narrow with sharp, arrow-shaped teeth, pike hide between the stems of underwater plants, silently waiting for victims. When a hapless fish, frog, snake, or duckling swims by, the pike will lunge forward and rip it to shreds.

## Singing Frogs, Snapping Turtles

Small tadpoles darting through a pond make an easy meal for a pike. And these creatures may be mistaken for fish, since they breathe through gills and live underwater. As they grow, however, tadpoles develop lungs and legs and turn into frogs. These creatures can be found in ponds throughout the world.

Frogs are hungry almost all the time and will eat just about anything, including insects, snails, tiny ducklings, and even other frogs. When they are not eating, frogs provide a musical symphony of croaking and chirping.

The spring peeper, found in the eastern United States and Canada, can inflate a balloonlike sack in its

*Frogs are born as tadpoles (inset). Tadpoles grow legs and their gills turn into lungs as they mature into frogs.*

neck and make a sharp, birdlike chirping song so loud it can be heard a mile away. On the other end of the musical scale, bullfrogs emit a low bass mooing that sounds like the words *jug-o'-rum*. Australia's giant tree frog is the largest frog in the world, with a body that can grow more than six inches long. The mating call of the giant tree frog sounds like a dog barking, but if it is distressed, the frog can screech like an unhappy cat.

Turtles are much quieter than frogs but just as common in a pond. In warm weather these hard-shelled creatures may often be seen in ponds throughout the world perched on logs or rocks basking in the sun. Like frogs, turtles are hungry creatures that will feed on bugs, tadpoles, aquatic plants, and dead organisms. The hungriest, however, is the snapping turtle, which can be found in Ecuador, Colombia, Mexico, and much of North America. Even when young and no bigger than a silver dollar, snapping turtles will use their powerful jaws to nip at anything that moves. When they grow up to weigh twenty-five to fifty pounds, snapping turtles will chomp down on fish, snakes, and even young muskrats. Snapping turtles will also bite humans, and people have lost fingers and toes to these bad-tempered turtles.

## Birds of the Pond

The natural habitat that ponds provide for turtles and other pond-dwellers is also highly prized by birds. The shores of ponds are lined with dried plants, grasses, and reeds that birds use to build nests. Pond waters provide these creatures with a place to drink, bathe, and eat.

Almost any pond will have its share of noisy ducks, geese, grebes, and other waterfowl. Depending on the pond's location, these birds may live in a pond year-round or visit only during the warm seasons. Mallard ducks, for example, can live in a partially frozen pond

# Creatures of a Pond

Red-
necked
Grebe

Bobcat

Water bug

Elk

Bullfrog

*Snow Geese feed on plants in a pond. Ponds support a wide variety of animals, all connected by the food chain.*

in winter as long as there is open water to search for food. Canada geese, however, fly to Mexico in the winter, stopping at ponds they find on their way south. In Australia and New Zealand, long-necked black swans fly through the sky in a V-shaped formation at over fifty miles per hour. When they land in ponds they honk and hiss as they swim about the water searching for plants to eat.

Many pond birds thrive on fish, frogs, and insects. Herons hunt while standing silently on one leg. When some food swims into sight, the long-necked bird lunges forward and grabs it with its beak. Fish eaters, such as the hawk, osprey, and kingfisher, swoop down out of the skies and grab fish with their razor-sharp claws called talons.

## Otters and Muskrats

Fur-bearing creatures, such as otters and raccoons, are at the top of the pond food chain and, when adults, have few natural enemies.

The lively otter, with species found in Africa, Asia, Europe, and North America, is the clown of the pond. These sleek creatures seem to make a game of whatever they are doing, whether swimming, walking on shore, frolicking in the snow, or hunting for food. Perhaps otters are carefree because their favorite foods—such as berries, roots, fish, salamanders, eels, worms, snails, and clams—are so abundant. With little worry as to where their next meal is coming from, otters have plenty of time to roll on the ground, wrestle, jump, and run.

Other **mammals** do not have it so easy. The muskrat, for example, remains busy building mound-like homes from cattails, branches, and other vegetation. Like the homes of their cousin the beaver, muskrat dens are engineering miracles full of dry chambers and tunnels.

Otters and muskrats are only two of the thousands of animals that inhabit ponds throughout the world. Some live within the pond their entire lives, others only visit. Like a bustling city with crowds of people, a tiny pond is a busy, buzzing center of activity for a diverse range of creatures.

# Chapter 4

# People and Ponds

**M**ost ponds exist less than one hundred years before they fill with silt and "die." This is part of the natural cycle of the pond. Someone driving a bulldozer, however, can bury a pond in a single day. Other activities, such as dumping pollution, can destroy a pond over several years.

Until recent decades people did not realize that ponds played a very important role in nature. Instead, these small bodies of water were often thought of as nuisances with mucky shores, snapping turtles, and clouds of blood-sucking mosquitoes. Such attitudes meant that people often used ponds as garbage dumps and sewers, or they were filled in to create farm fields or building sites.

# Beavers and Floods

Perhaps the largest widespread destruction of ponds took place in North America between 1600 and 1850. During those years beaver furs were used to make hats, coats, and other clothing. To fulfill the demand

*People once dumped garbage into ponds. Today, people understand the value of ponds and are working to create new ones.*

for beaver pelts, tens of thousands of trappers hunted beaver along nearly every river and stream in America. As a result the population of beavers fell from about 200 million in 1700 to near zero by the mid-1800s.

With the animals gone there were no more natural dams, and beaver ponds disappeared. This, in turn, reduced the habitat for millions of other creatures, such as fish, game animals, and waterfowl. With no natural beaver ponds to slow the flow of water, towns built near rivers were flooded more often and sometimes more severely.

Beaver hats fell out of fashion in the nineteenth century, and the population of animals began to slowly rebound. Today, however, beavers are considered bothersome by many landowners because ponds fill the areas behind their dams, often flooding valuable farm, ranch, or forest land. While some farmers trap beaver in order to stop such problems, the animals are protected in some states by environmental laws.

## Ponds and Farming

Farmers affect natural ponds in other ways. Sometimes ponds are used by livestock for water. When this happens the hooves of heavy cows, horses, and other animals trample and destroy plants in the swamp zone. When ponds are used to water crops, they are often drained quickly and turn into dry holes.

Perhaps the most troublesome problem, however, is the widespread use of fertilizers on farm fields.

*Cows graze near a pond. Livestock often trample and destroy the plant life surrounding ponds.*

Agricultural fertilizers are helpful for growing crops and are also used on lawns, home gardens, and golf courses. These chemicals, however, wash into ponds when it rains. Fertilizers that make corn grow tall also cause algae and other pond plants to grow rapidly and uncontrollably. Algae blooms block sunlight from reaching the bottom of the pond, causing the death of plants such as water lilies. When the algae eventually dies, it lowers oxygen levels to a point at which plants and animals die.

# Mosquito Control

In some cases people have purposely sprayed harmful chemicals into ponds. This is most often done to kill mosquitoes. While these chemicals have controlled the numbers of the sometimes disease-carrying insects, there has been a price to pay for this benefit.

The chemical DDT is a good example of a substance made by humans that has seriously affected ponds. People began spraying DDT into ponds to kill mosquitoes in the 1950s. This chemical was considered a miracle in Africa, South America, and elsewhere as the number of mosquito-related deaths from malaria and other diseases dropped rapidly wherever it was used.

Soon people began using DDT in colder climates, where there was no threat of malaria, simply because mosquitoes were a nuisance. By the late 1950s the chemical began showing up in the flesh of fish. Birds that ate the fish, such as grebes, hawks, and other pond-dwellers, suffered ill effects. Because of DDT their egg shells became so thin that they broke easily and fewer chicks were born. By the 1960s bird species, such as peregrine falcons, were threatened with extinction.

In the 1960s, when DDT was discovered in human beings, the chemical was banned in the United States. It is still used, with negative side effects on wildlife and humans, in many countries where malaria is a problem.

Pesticides that replaced DDT in North America have had an equally harmful effect on pond organisms. For example, in 1995 researchers in Minnesota discovered frogs born with deformed or misshapen legs, or missing one eye. Since that time deformed frogs have been discovered in forty-two states and in many places in Canada. Scientists believe that this is a result of frogs absorbing toxic chemicals through their skin that harms the way they reproduce.

*This five-legged frog is deformed because of chemicals in its pond water. Thousands of pond creatures are deformed as a result of pollution.*

# Growing Population

While chemical pollution threatens ponds in rural (country) areas, thousands of these fragile, freshwater pools are disappearing every year due to agriculture, construction, and development.

The number of people on Earth has doubled from 3 billion to more than 6 billion since 1960. This grow-

*A man and his grandchild use a net to fish in a pond. Humans play the most important role in the future of the earth's ponds.*

ing population needs homes, schools, hospitals, factories, shopping centers, and new places to grow food. In crowded countries such as China, Thailand, and India, few natural ponds exist. Instead, these bodies of water have been converted for use as aquatic farms where companies grow rice and raise fish and shrimp for food production.

When ponds stand in the way of city and town expansion, they are often destroyed to make way for development. Since they are small, and often unnamed, no organization can keep track of the number of ponds destroyed every year by development.

Fortunately ponds can be created as well as destroyed. In Great Britain, where 75 percent of all natural pools have been lost to development in the last century, a government program has encouraged people to create new ponds. In the town of Carron Dams, Scotland, over thirty-three volunteers spent nearly two months creating a pond by hand, using shovels and wheelbarrows to remove dirt. It was naturally filled by rainwater and stocked with fish by workers. This pond is only one of twenty thousand constructed in Great Britain between 1990 and 2000. Although they are made by people, these quiet pools quickly attract wildlife, including beetles, frogs, herons, and aquatic plants.

## An Important Role

As long as humans have lived near ponds, they have shaped, changed, and sometimes destroyed them.

*The sun rises over a quiet pond. Ponds are an important part of the earth's ecology.*

The forests around ponds have been cut down, the rivers that fed them diverted, and the animals that lived in them hunted. Yet freshwater ponds continue to play an extremely important role in the ecology of the earth. They provide feeding and nesting stations for countless creatures, help prevent flooding, and filter pollution from water. Perhaps just as important in the busy, modern world, ponds are peaceful places where nature's cycles can continue uninterrupted. In a world where wilderness areas are shrinking by the day, ponds offer great benefits to plants, animals, and people throughout the world.

# Glossary

**aquatic:** Living or growing in or on water.

**dam:** A natural or human-made barrier across a waterway that blocks the flow of water and creates a pond or lake behind it.

**environment:** Conditions that affect and influence the growth, development, and survival of plants and animals.

**fresh water:** Water found in ponds, lakes, and rivers that is not salty like seawater.

**glacier:** A huge mass of ice made from compressed snow that moves slowly over land.

**habitat:** The area or type of environment in which an organism normally lives.

**mammal:** Warm-blooded creatures that have a covering of hair and whose young are born alive and nourished by their mothers' milk.

**nutrient:** A mineral or chemical that provides a source of nourishment, especially in food.

**organism:** An individual form of life, such as a plant or an animal.

**photosynthesis:** The process by which green plants convert energy from sunlight into food and oxygen.

**predator:** An animal that lives by preying on other animals.

**species:** A category or type of plant or animal.

**submerged:** Growing or remaining underwater.

# For Further Exploration

Katya Arnold, *Let's Find It!: My First Nature Guide*. New York: Holiday House, 2002. Presents pictures of such varied environments as a forest, a street, a spring garden, the beach, and a pond, with labels to identify different plants and animals.

Ellen Doris, *Woods, Ponds, and Fields*. Danbury, CT: Grolier, 1996. This book is a field guide for exploring the outdoors, with projects, field trips, ideas, and suggestions for learning about the ecology of plants and animals in ponds, forests, and fields.

Adam Hibbert, *A Freshwater Pond*. New York: Crabtree, 1999. A book about ponds and the creepy, crawly insects and larger animals found in their waters.

Isaac Nadeau, *Food Chains in a Pond Habitat*. New York: PowerKids, 2002. The story of how big creatures eat smaller ones in the pond environment. The book traces the food chain from tiny water insects to large hawks and otters.

Donald Silver, *One Small Square: Pond*. New York: W.H. Freeman, 1994. This book covers the wide variety of plants and animals found in a small area of a pond, from the surface of the water to the mud on the bottom.

David Stewart, *Pond Life*. New York: Franklin Watts, 2002. A simple introduction to the life and life cycles of pond animals throughout the year.

# Index

# Picture Credits

Cover: PhotoDisc

© Theo Allofs/CORBIS, 17

© Carolina Biological/Visuals Unlimited, 19 (inset)

COREL Corporation, 9, 11, 22, 24, 27, 29
  (lower left)

© Darrell Gulin/CORBIS, 30

Chris Jouan, 15, 29

© Lindsay Hebberd/CORBIS, 38

© Carol Hughes, Gallo Images/CORBIS, 25

© Pat O'Hara/CORBIS, 5

PhotoDisc, 13 (inset), 15, 29 (all but lower left), 35

© James Randklev/CORBIS, 19

© Bob Rowan, Progressive Image/CORBIS, 6

© Phil Schermeister/CORBIS, 13

© Mark Smith/Photo Researchers, 37

© Joseph Sohm, ChromoSohm, Inc./CORBIS, 40

© Inga Spence/Visuals Unlimited, 33

© Steve Watson, 27 (inset)

# About the Author

Stuart A. Kallen is the author of more than 160 non-fiction books for children and young adults. He has written on topics ranging from the theory of relativity to the history of rock and roll. In addition he has written award-winning children's videos and television scripts. In his spare time he is a singer/songwriter/guitarist in San Diego, California.

Comsewogue Public Library
170 Terryville Road
Port Jefferson Station, NY 11776